EVERYONE IS MULTICULTURAL

EVERYONE IS MULTICULTURAL

✦

Bridging Cultural Influences for Leadership Success

Dr. Pamela Johnson

iUniverse, Inc.
New York Lincoln Shanghai

EVERYONE IS MULTICULTURAL
Bridging Cultural Influences for Leadership Success

iUniverse books may be ordered through booksellers or by contacting:

iUniverse
2021 Pine Lake Road, Suite 100
Lincoln, NE 68512
www.iuniverse.com
1-800-Authors (1-800-288-4677)

ISBN-13: 978-0-595-38518-8 (pbk)
ISBN-13: 978-0-595-82899-9 (ebk)
ISBN-10: 0-595-38518-4 (pbk)
ISBN-10: 0-595-82899-X (ebk)

Printed in the United States of America

Contents

About the Author ix

Introduction xi

      "What Are We Doing Wrong?"

CHAPTER 1   The Diversity Awareness Movement 1

CHAPTER 2   The Coaching Movement 8

CHAPTER 3   Past Approaches. 12

CHAPTER 4   Everyone Is Multicultural 15

CHAPTER 5   The Power of Unique Cultural Influences 19

CHAPTER 6   Multicultural Leadership Development 26

CHAPTER 7   Multicultural Self-Awareness and Growth 32

CHAPTER 8   Multicultural Awareness of Others 39

CHAPTER 9   Multicultural Leadership Skill Development and
                  Adjustment 43

CHAPTER 10   The Multicultural Leadership Development
                  Process. 49

Acknowledgements

My deepest gratitude goes to my many individual and organizational multicultural clients. We have learned about each other and have grown together in an effort not only to become better people and organizations, but also to impact the beginning of a better world.

I would also like to thank my wonderful husband Nathan, and sons Evan and Aaryn. It is because of you that I continue to find meaning in the work that I do. You give me the strength and support that make life enjoyable.

And lastly, I would like to thank my mom and dad. You have allowed me to experience many cultural influences.

About the Author

Dr. Pamela Johnson is an expert in multicultural leadership development with more than twenty years of experience as a practitioner, educator, trainer, and consultant. As a private practitioner, Dr. Johnson has successfully facilitated multicultural individual and group counseling and coaching. As an educator, she is a university professor teaching master's-level courses in multicultural counseling, career counseling, and human behavior and development. As a trainer and consultant, Dr. Johnson has worked with private and public organizational executives, leadership candidates, and staff on cultural and gender diversity, multicultural leadership development, and discrimination/harassment issues.

Dr. Johnson is an author whose most recent article, "Diversititis…Is there a cure?", has been published in numerous magazines including *Minority Business News USA*, *Women's Enterprise*, *Diversity Texas*, and *Minority Business News Texas*. She is also the author of *AIDS and African Americans*.

Dr. Johnson has developed the Cultural Continuum Theory and Corporate Kaleidoscope™, components of a multicultural leadership development process. She is an international speaker and trainer. Dr. Johnson presented at the International Association of Career Firms 2004 Conference in Prague, Czech Republic. She believes that while the organization has a responsibility to develop and implement diversity initiatives, that responsibility is within each and every member of the organization at every level. She says, "Each individual must 'get

honest' with themselves and take responsibility for their own stereotypes, bias and behaviors."

Dr. Johnson holds a Bachelor of Arts degree in communications, a
Master of Arts degree in human behavior and business, a Master of Science degree in counseling and guidance, and a Doctorate Degree of
Education, majoring in counseling and guidance with a minor in business management. She is a certified dispute mediator, a licensed professional counselor by the state of Texas, and a national certified
counselor.

Introduction

✦

"What Are We Doing Wrong?"

Two senior human resources executives of a Fortune 100 company called on me to discuss several talent-management problems they were having within their company. These two executives were committed to the success of their company and to the successful development of a "model" multicultural organization.

They knew the potential financial impact that an effective diversity initiative could have on the future of their company. They also knew the intrinsic value a successful diversity initiative would add to the management, satisfaction, and productivity of the thousands of employees in their organization. These two HR professionals were also sensitive to the unique needs of culturally diverse employees and honestly seemed to care about their happiness within the organization.

This particular company, like many other large businesses between 2000 and 2005, was attempting to address the critical need to become a truly diverse and inclusive corporation. They had finally embraced the reality that not only was it the right thing to do but it also made good business sense.

It seemed that despite all of their efforts to deliver a successful diversity initiative, one that would be inclusive of culturally diverse representation in all levels of the organization, they were still having a few difficulties. Their primary complaint was their inability to meet the corporate goal of having a team of senior managers and executives who were culturally diverse.

This company's human resources team had had a reasonable amount of success in recruiting and hiring culturally diverse individuals into entry-level management positions. They only hired the best and brightest in their fields. But for many reasons, this organization continued to struggle to retain these candidates for longer than a few years. They said they had tried everything. They had invested vast amounts of time and money into these candidates by offering above-average benefits, competitive salaries, state-of-the-art training, and varying degrees of managerial experience—all designed to help increase employee retention rates and leadership development.

The human resources team of this company assumed that if they could keep their culturally diverse employees and work with them for a few more years, they would be able to groom these individuals for senior management positions. The company had previously developed and implemented state-of-the-art diversity training programs, coaching programs, and mentoring programs. But the retention problems remained, reducing the company's ability to promote more culturally diverse candidates.

Interestingly enough, the company did have limited success with its programs designed to promote the inclusion of women into leadership positions. In fact, the company was pleased with its ability to hire, retain, and promote women. The human resources executives were also pleased with the level of female representation they had achieved in the organization's executive ranks. Most of their initiatives for the inclusion of women were working. They subsequently tried to mirror some of these programs with other cultural groups but, again, to no avail. The leadership development programs they had implemented for women were not working for other cultural groups.

These two well-meaning and, I might add, fairly culturally sensitive and knowledgeable HR professionals were at their wits' end. They simply did not know what else to do. They did not know what they were doing wrong. They just wanted to know how they could retain more people of color long enough to develop their management skills and integrate them into the system, similar to the way they had integrated women.

The discussion I had with these professionals led me to write this book. They wanted to know why their cultural diversity programs had failed. Basically they wanted to know, "Why are well-trained, skilled, culturally diverse candidates still leaving?" And more importantly, they wanted to know what needed to be done differently and how to develop an effective multicultural leadership program.

This multicultural leadership retention and development dilemma is not unique to this company. It is a problem that many large-and medium-sized corporations, businesses, and institutions continue to struggle with on a daily basis. These same organizations are all too often guided by strategic plans with measurable goals for improved diversity processes and results, including the number of multicultural executives.

To top it all off, these organizations are getting additional political, consumer, and social pressure to have an organization that looks like society at large. Pressure for corporate diversity can come from government requirements, as well as from global competition. And of course, let us not overlook the few well-meaning company leaders who are simply trying to do the right thing but still having similar challenges.

The mass hiring and promotion of women has been the saving grace for many of these organizations for years. Hence, it makes sense that more women, although still a limited number, have now gained presence in executive ranks. This progression was simply due to the availability of a significantly large population of women and a large proportion of women in the workforce. Human resource professionals were able to choose from an increased pool of female candidates that could easily be refilled if needed.

By having the sheer number and availability of qualified women, organizations have had the time for effective leadership grooming and therefore subsequent promotion. And because women have been considered a minority group for years, many businesses' diversity programs have been successful at increasing diversity compliance.

But today, the focus of diversity has changed. Due to globalization and technological advances, the shift is beyond gender, race, and country of origin. The shift is beyond quotas and numbers. And more importantly, the shift is even beyond education and skill levels. The term "diversity" has been broadened into multidimensional aspects including the diversity of psychological, behavioral, and emotional styles. "Diversity" has to include not only cultural values and beliefs but also the impact of history, family, and economics. The desire for a truly inclusive organization has to come from not only the structure and strategic plan of the organization but from within the hearts and minds of the individual leadership candidates and leadership teams.

1

The Diversity Awareness Movement

The buzz words for corporate America in the 1990s were "cultural diversity," "diversity awareness," and "cultural sensitivity." Although the terms were new, the basic concepts and issues at hand were not new to the United States. In fact, with the exception of Native Americans, everyone in the United States originally emigrated from other countries, spoke various languages, had different customs, and had different ways of doing things.

The United States has always been made up of people with various religions, customs, behaviors, practices, beliefs, values, and worldviews. With respect to the world of work and work ethics, these same individuals also have many different views on working, communicating, building relationships, and collaborating with others. So, one would think that after over 300 hundred years of multiculturalism in America, individuals would be proportionately represented in every aspect of American life, including the leadership and executive ranks. Unfortunately, even in the present year, this inevitability is not so.

One of the primary consequences that separated the prestigiously successful individual from the unsuccessful, besides socioeconomics and language, was the obvious physical characteristics that varied from one cultural group to another. The color of skin, the texture of hair, the body size and shape, the shape of eyes, nose, and even face were readily used to discriminate the ones who were unworthy of status and position from the ones who were worthy. The earliest settlers with power and money were of European descent. Hence, the standards of physical and intellectual acceptance were based on European characteristics and subsequently passed on from generation to generation.

These Europeans may have been from different countries and may have spoken different languages, but they often had similar physical characteristics. They often looked alike. With the adjustment of perhaps their language, they could easily blend in with the existing power structure.

Due to great prejudice and discrimination in those times, those who wanted to become successful had to hide their cultural identities, learn to live two culturally different lives, or give up their original cultural identities and adopt the cultural identity and behaviors of those in power. Some could simply change their names, languages, and religions to avoid potential discrimination and roadblocks that would prevent them from becoming successful in a booming and industrialized country.

These same people were also becoming America's citizens, customers, employees, and managers. Theoretically, the more different a person looked, acted, sounded, and behaved from the "White Anglo Saxon Protestant," the harder it was for them to blend in, even if they wanted to, and the more likely they were to have problems in rising to higher positions in organizations and institutions.

Consequently, individuals of African, Asian, and Spanish descent would magnify diversity issues. These people would have extreme difficulty at physically blending in, especially since the standards, rules, stereotypes, and attitudes had already been set and accepted by mainstream society. Along with these "different looking" people came different attitudes, beliefs, values, history, pride, and motivation.

Mainstream U.S. society subsequently began to develop increased fear, anxiety, prejudice, hatred, sexism, and racism. Furthermore, for these individuals, blending in physically was not a possibility, and for most, blending in was not even a desire.

In the 1950s and 1960s, participating in traditional corporate and institutional practices of exclusivity and segregation was not an option for these culturally diverse groups. Individuals were unable to change their physical characteristics and not willing to change their cultural ways of thinking, feeling, and behaving. But they were still very capable and valuable assets for any organization.

Social and political pressure from the civil rights movement and the women's rights movement forced organizations to make employment adjustments in favor of various groups. These diverse groups included people of a different color or of a different country of origin, various religious groups, and women, just to name a few. In order for a company to remain competitive, as well as in legal compliance with the Civil Rights Act and affirmative action requirements, it was critical for businesses and other American institutions to attract, hire, and retain these now legally protected culturally diverse groups of people.

The school of thought at that time became a matter of numbers, and many organizations sought to meet quotas. Organizations looked to hire women and minorities to fulfill affirmative action requirements. The mentality was that this was a necessary initiative to rectify past injustices and the inequalities of the American workforce. For many organizations, due to still overwhelming prejudice and discrimination, this forced legal requirement was believed to be the best way for the American workforce to quickly achieve integration.

For all practical purposes, the Civil Rights Act and affirmative action requirements did what they were supposed to do. Many women and members of various minority groups were and still are hired into the

American workforce. And today, the "numbers game" is not as much of an issue for organizations as it was in the past. But this is not the end of the story.

In the 1990s, many new questions began to surface, such as:

- How does the organization maintain retention, especially when prejudice and in-house discrimination continue to occur?

- How can we reduce some of the institutional barriers of sexism and racism in higher levels of the organization?

- How can we improve upon the quality of relationships between people who have different views of the world?

- How can we improve upon the happiness and satisfaction of such a diverse workforce?

- How can we increase minority representation in all levels and departments of the organization?

- How does the organization continue to profit and grow with such a diverse workforce?

- How do we increase the customer base in diverse populations and communities?

- How do we improve our image?

One of the best ways to successfully address these questions was for these organizations and their employees to focus on employee emotional and intellectual well-being. It was not enough to hire and provide a good salary with good benefits. Employee well-being would include such concerns as happiness, comfort, satisfaction, respect, appreciation, fairness, prestige, understanding, and promotions, just to name a few. Organizations needed to focus on much more than the satisfaction of the culturally diverse employees, but on the satisfaction of all employees.

Generally, most individuals who are not valued, respected, and appreciated, regardless of pay and benefits, will either leave the organization or become less committed, ineffective, or unproductive. When this occurs, the organization loses a huge investment of training, expertise, skills, knowledge, and productivity.

In many cases, this loss bleeds into other areas, such as the morale, spirit, happiness, and productivity of the remaining workers. For a company to truly survive, it has to learn how to reduce turnover (and in some cases, reduce discrimination claims and lawsuits) and learn how to address the diverse needs of a diverse employee and customer base.

Hence, organizations started the new wave of human capital management and the beginning of the cultural diversity agenda. Early cultural diversity initiatives were based on diversity-awareness training for everyone in the organization. This was a viable and very important beginning. Most of this training was designed to help employees gain a deeper appreciation for the value that a diverse workforce brings to a company and a society as a whole.

Effective diversity-awareness training provided basic information to help broaden understanding of different worldviews and values, while exploring the commonalities of human nature. Most of these trainings, if properly conducted, helped broaden the knowledge, understanding, acceptance, and tolerance for differences between major cultural groups, as well as some of the differences between employees. In some cases, company policies were changed to respect different cultural values, such as dress, holidays, and celebrations.

As time passed and more employees of diverse backgrounds began to join the work force, it was soon discovered that diversity-awareness training was not enough to break the barriers of fear, discomfort, mistrust, prejudice, and discrimination, especially when it came to the hiring and promotion of culturally diverse individuals into higher levels of management.

Even well-meaning directors and executives struggled with acceptance and understanding of what it meant to a company to have not only diversity in the lower ranks but also in the executive ranks. So the corporate diversity initiative had to be directed toward not only attracting, hiring, and retaining culturally diverse employees but also promotion, respect, and acceptance.

To make matters even more difficult, many of the culturally diverse employees, who were highly educated, trained, and very effective at their jobs had very little knowledge about or experience with higher-level corporate culture, including its values, beliefs, and customs.

Just like any ethnic, religious, or other cultural group, each American corporate culture has its own set of norms and rules that are both spoken and unspoken. If a person wants to successfully join that culture, he or she either has to change the rules, which is often impossible, or has to learn, understand, and function effectively within those cultural boundaries.

Unfortunately, many of these early diversity programs failed. Often the primary focus was one-way with a "we understand them" mentality. These programs usually focused on how the mainstream employees could learn about the values, behaviors, and beliefs of the people who were the minority.

These programs rarely talked about the values, behaviors, and beliefs of the people who were the majority and how people could adapt without giving up who they are. Although informative, these programs were rarely personalized. The uniqueness of the individual's personality, behaviors, values, and beliefs was seldom addressed.

These programs were a disservice to individuals who were new to this society or new to the American corporate culture. They also did very little to help the employee manage stress, anxiety, and adjustment into mainstream corporate culture. These culturally different employees were left to figure things out in the only way they knew how—from their cultural worldview.

Although adjustment and success would eventually be achieved, it was often difficult and, more importantly, time-consuming. And when an individual is working up the corporate ladder, timing is everything.

2

The Coaching Movement

Two new buzzwords for many corporations at the turn of the century were "coaching" and "mentoring". They were beginning to realize the importance of having minorities and women in the higher ranks of the organization, and they wanted them in position as soon as realistically possible.

Not only did promotions make good business sense, but they were good for employees' motivation and morale and a good marketing tool for the growing minority customer base. The glass ceiling was a reality that needed to be addressed and rectified.

Interestingly enough, because of the increased levels of diversity throughout American universities, colleges, technical schools, and other institutions of higher learning, the issues in employment were not about the education, ability, or skills of minority individuals making it to the top. Instead, the issue was how these very capable individuals could achieve business performance goals as well as learn the corporate culture so they could better fit in and subsequently be accepted into top executive positions.

The focus of many corporate diversity initiatives for promoting minorities into higher management ranks turned toward helping individuals understand and appreciate the organization's corporate culture, rather than focusing on the individual's culture. The thought was that the corporations should spend time and money to help the leadership candidate understand and accept the organization's values, beliefs, customs, language, politics, procedures, and systems.

Again, well-meaning human resource professionals were asked to implement coaching programs and mentoring programs where supervisors and managers were expected to guide their employees individually to improve their personal and company goals and performance. The manager and employee were to meet periodically and discuss goals, problems, and issues and develop ways the candidate could succeed. The manager was to give direction and information about what might work best in the particular environment or for a particular situation. The coach or mentor was thought to have insight and information that would help the candidate better understand the corporate culture and ways of doing things and therefore help them learn more quickly how to "play the game."

These programs were also designed to help employees who were unfamiliar with the American corporate culture, and more specifically the culture of a particular organization, fit in better and conform. The hope was that if an employee could be a top performer and learn how to navigate the organization's culture, that person would stand a better chance of success.

For a corporation to quickly accomplish this goal, the development of new coaching and mentoring initiatives began. In some cases, these programs were also implemented for specific high-potential, and often minority, leadership candidates. Some candidates were even put in fast-track programs, earmarking them for advancement within the company.

Such programs were also designed to provide candidates with a one-on-one relationship with someone who had more knowledge and insight about the organization's inner workings. This person was to coach the candidate in order to better succeed and potentially move up the corporate ladder. In some situations, as not to discriminate against white men, coaching programs were developed for all candidates, not just minority candidates.

The coaching/mentor process, although very important and often helpful, usually had several major drawbacks. First, the process was designed to help individuals learn about the corporate culture and essentially learn to do things "the corporate way" or more specifically "our way." And similar to the diversity-awareness process that had a mentality of "us understanding them," the coaching process was also one-way: the mentality was "them understanding the corporation." This mirrored blending—in, but the blending was psychological, rather than physical. The message was, "If you do it the same way we do it, you are more likely to succeed."

The second major drawback was that the coach or mentor's level of diversity knowledge and sensitivity needed to be examined. In many cases the coach still had significant issues of bias, prejudice, stereotypes, and covert discrimination thereby limiting the effectiveness of the coaching process. Often, these coaches did not realize their limitations. The coach needed to be a good match with the employee.

Unfortunately, the mentors often knew very little about the impact that their cultural influences might have on an individual's behaviors and life. These employees were trying to understand the corporate culture through someone else's eyes instead of through their own cultural filters.

Consequently, the result would be a mentor advising a person to do things the corporate way and in ways that might have worked for the mentor in the past, but that might not fit the employee's worldview, cultural values, or work habits.

A third drawback was that for any coaching program to be effective the parties involved had to have a comfortable and trusting relationship. The individuals needed to be open and honest and willing to talk about issues that could be blocking the candidate's progression up the corporate ladder, including cultural issues.

Many candidates may not have felt comfortable discussing such personal thoughts and feelings. Both parties had to be willing to conduct self-examinations and openly discuss how they really felt about themselves, each other, cultural issues, the organization, other employees, attitudes and behaviors, and how they could work together. What worked for one person's advancement may not work for another. If the unique cultural influences were ignored, effective adjustments would be difficult to make.

The coaching and mentoring process, like that of diversity-awareness training, was very much needed and crucial in the diversity initiatives of corporate America. But the programs also fell short, because their mentality was "you understand us." If the individual was willing to do things the organization's way, the belief was, they would be more likely to succeed. Furthermore, the coaching process was presumptive in the thought that if it had worked for the coach or mentor in the past, it would work for someone new.

Lastly, many minorities in America seem to struggle with living bicultural lives. It is often difficult and stressful to perform and behave in one worldview forty to fifty hours a week at work, and then to switch gears to another worldview outside of work. Most of the time the adjustment and daily challenges are manageable, but sometimes the two worlds collide, affecting one's lifestyle, family relationships, religious practices, and ability to perform effectively.

Balancing life with home and work is hard enough without having to live two distinct cultural lives. Individuals should be able to remain who they are fundamentally and culturally, while making some adjustments to meet the needs of the business and of their careers.

3

Past Approaches

Many organizations have attempted to adjust to the demands of a diverse workforce and customer base for decades. These attempts have often resulted in ineffective hiring and retention efforts and compromised senior-level and executive promotions. In addition, these attempts have often resulted in employee dissatisfaction and low productivity, negative customer and public perception, and of course, struggling profits and growth.

We have seen antidiscrimination laws, affirmative action programs, diversity-awareness training, coaching and mentoring initiatives, and even headquarter directives. Unquestionably, these programs and initiatives have been important and often critically needed in most organizations. But historically, each of these approaches to solving the corporate diversity dilemma was thought to be the best approach for success at that point.

The primary problem was that each program had a unidirectional approach to solving complex diversity issues. This approach is often "the company vs. the people," and it is because of this that many of the initiatives are not working as expected.

We have to look at all of the affected responsible parties and all of the contributing factors. In fact, we have to use a multidirectional approach where many things, including people and processes, impact the outcome of diversity endeavors. An effective diverse corporation is a functional system, much like the human body. Each part of the system has a responsibility that contributes to the overall health. If a single part is not functioning properly, it can impact the entire system.

With that in mind, let's take a deeper look at some of today's traditional diversity approaches. One school of thought is that workforce diversity is a 'majority-to-minority' issue. Generally, this concept consists of well-meaning corporations that have been led for decades by white men steadily trying to fix diversity concerns by adding more minority representation. A truly diverse workforce initiative must be all-inclusive.

The workforce must be made up of many types of people at every level who have the capacity and ability to fulfill corporate requirements. Majority-to-minority concepts are limiting and undermine the corporation's full potential. A diverse corporate base includes people from various countries, regions, and religions; people with varying beliefs, values, and work ethics; people with different socioeconomic, childhood, and adult experiences; people with language and communication differences; people with different personalities; and many more. Diversity goes beyond gender, race, or country of origin.

Another contemporary view in dealing with diversity issues is that organizations are responsible for complying with regulations or developing strategic diversity programs and services, often forced by legal or social demands. Once again, this is a limited view. The corporation plays a major role in diversity initiative development and implementation, as well as providing opportunities for their employees, but that responsibility also lies within each and every member of the organization at every level.

Everyone must own up to their part played in the corporation's diversity initiatives. Individuals must be honest with themselves and take responsibility for their own stereotypes, biases, and behaviors. Too many times have I seen individuals expect their company to do the right thing for employees when they personally don't do the right thing when working with others.

A third view is that employees need to learn about each other and value diversity only at work. Just because a company makes everyone go through a diversity training program focused on the workplace, it does not mean it is going to make a difference in leadership development and promotion. The workplace is *not* the only place diversity counts. It should be valued everywhere!

It is no secret that Sunday morning is the most segregated time in the United States. We must learn to value diversity at the mall, at church, in politics, and everywhere we go. And for corporations, it is not just about valuing the diversity of employees. It is about valuing the diverse customer, vendor, local and global community, and all of society. A truly successful leadership development program must include the dedicated and genuine efforts of everyone in the organization, including the candidates and the existing leaders.

4

Everyone Is Multicultural

As a consultant specializing in workforce diversity, I am often called on by organizational leaders to help them with employee diversity issues. The calls are most frequently from human resources leaders who are struggling to manage diverse employees. Problems range from inappropriate employee behaviors, including name-calling and the use of racial slurs, to hiring and discrimination.

Let's begin by examining a couple of the current perceptions and misconceptions about cultural diversity. It never ceases to amaze me how many people in today's workforce, including human resources professionals, leadership teams, and employees, still have a limited view of this concept.

One of the most common views of diversity is that it is still a numbers game. I often get calls regarding recruitment and hiring for people of color. For some organizations, this may be one of the problems that needs to be addressed, but it's certainly not the only problem that needs to be addressed. Many leaders still believe that once they have hired enough people of color and they are in federal compliance, their diversity problem will be solved.

Another view of diversity is that it has to do only with the employees who are non-white. Many individuals still view diversity as a racial or ethnic issue. Of course, race and ethnicity have a role in the process, but again, this is only part of the issue. Even if an organization employs people of all races and ethnicities, they may still have diversity issues.

I believe each and every individual is culturally diverse from every other person. More specifically, I believe that everyone is multicultural. It is not just about race or ethnicity. My contention is that everyone has a unique culture made up of many sub-cultural influences, and these cultural influences help make them who they are. For one to assume that a person might believe a certain thing or behave a certain way because of race, country of origin, or religion is a gross overgeneralization of what that person might be like.

I believe some people may be impacted by one cultural influence more than another and may follow most of the cultural norms of that dominating cultural group. But in reality, most people are impacted by many cultural influences and in varying combinations depending on the situation. Therefore, no two people can be of the same culture.

Even identical twins raised by the same parents in the same environment cannot have all of the same cultural influences. Each twin has different life experiences and, based on their perceptions of these experiences, may have different beliefs and values, all of which are part of one's cultural life.

Culture has to do with everything that makes a person who they are. It often has to do with the influence of race, country of origin, ethnicity, gender, and religion. But it also has to do with upbringing, the ethnic and family history, current and past relationships, and how the person views the world around him or her. Culture has to do with customs, traditions, values, and significant events. But it also has to do with economic status, personality, education, age, and personal experiences. Cultural influence has to do with how people dress, dance, and what music they enjoy. But it also has to do with how they communicate, socialize, work, love, and even hate. The list goes on and on. The point is that everyone is culturally diverse from everyone else, and everyone has many cultural influences.

A person might be born Anglo, but grew up Catholic, is a senior citizen, is hearing impaired, and has lived most of life in an urban city in South Africa. This same person may have a French mother, an American father, and nine siblings. This is just an example, but the point is that very few people are members of just one culture group and therefore should be viewed accordingly.

To really get to know and understand any individual from a cultural perspective, one would have to learn which cultures and cultural influences play dominant roles in the person's life. We could be wrong, inappropriate, and even disrespectful if we made assumptions about a person because of the cultural groups they belong to without finding out more about that person from their perspective.

Considering this uniqueness, we can look at how much impact the dominating cultural influence might have on a person. The above-mentioned person may be impacted the most at work by being in the hearing-impaired culture. If so, how might his life, including his work life, be different by being in the deaf culture? How might he behave? How might this affect relationships with co-workers? What might be of value? How might the person see the world and others? Race, country of origin, and religion may be of comparably little influence to this person when at work.

But what about when the person is at home? Being a part of the deaf culture may be less of an influence, and the impact of his religion may kick in. This is just an example, but it should help us understand that culture is important. However, we should not limit ourselves with one view and ignore the multiplicity of what diversity means. If we truly want to respect and appreciate people's differences, we have to go beyond what we see when we look at them.

The next question is what are the many cultures that influence a person's life? Which culture plays a bigger part in her life and under what circumstances? And with respect to the world of work, which cultural influences impact a person's work ethic, relationships and perspectives on leadership? What are her work-related values and beliefs based on? How does culture play a role in her concepts of time, teamwork, communication, authority, discipline, and feedback? Is it a combination of many cultures or is it just a few? It is unfair to box people into cultural norms simply by what we see, hear, or read.

For some, the variance of cultural influences might not be large. For some, their lives may primarily be influenced by their devout religious beliefs and practices, where little else may matter. For others, their lives may primarily be influenced by their racial and family history, events, and practices, where little else may matter. In these cases, the lines are clearer, and some of the rules, norms, and values are easier to apply. But for the most part, true cultural diversity is about the impact various cultures have had on that person to make them who they are.

Everyone is made up of many cultures and is multicultural. The more a specific culture has influenced a person, the more likely it is that others need to know and understand that culture. We have to stop making assumptions about a person's culture and cultural influences simply based on what we see. More importantly, we have to stop making decisions and practicing certain behaviors based on those assumptions. Sometimes we could be right, but many times we could be wrong.

Furthermore, everyone should be included in cultural diversity initiatives, training programs, and processes. Organizational leaders are doing themselves and the organization an injustice when they leave out the cultural values and differences everyone brings to the organization.

5

The Power of Unique Cultural Influences

In 1969 my family and I moved to a small Texas town, just east of Houston. I was a 12-year-old, African American (then referenced as Black) female in the eighth grade attending a predominately white school for the first time. One of America's diversity issues at that time was integration. It was the physical, legal, and social integration of children and adults who were of different races into the same schools, restaurants, stores, corporations, and other institutions.

The United States' answer to the social ills of the multicultural 1960s was mixing races through integration. The hope, aside from getting rid of discrimination, was that if people could learn to work and function together, they would eventually learn to appreciate and respect one another. Fortunately, over a period of forty to fifty years, this process is slowly working.

Nevertheless, one might have thought that at this particular time in my life relocating into a predominately white school and neighborhood would have been a difficult adjustment. One also might have thought that this adjustment would have been filled with struggles, barriers, and discrimination. Others might have even thought that I would have had difficulty making friends, fitting in, gaining acceptance, or excelling academically. I even remember my parents trying to prepare me for the prejudice and discrimination that might occur.

But my worldview, experiences, and cultural influences were different. In fact, I was quite comfortable and adjusted quite easily. I was even the only black female in my junior high school to make the high school drill team. Ironically, I had never seen the drill team before and knew nothing about it.

I never wondered why or how I was able to succeed in this new and different environment until now. I was a typical A-B student who always had to study hard to get good grades. I had no special musical skills or dance training and certainly did not have rich parents. So how was I able to do it? What was it that made the difference?

Before moving to this town and attending this school, my dad had been in the army, and I was born and lived on many different army bases all of my life. Subsequently, I attended schools with other kids whose dads were also in the army. We were affectionately called "army brats." Most of the schools, churches, and stores we went to were also on or near the base. There was no such thing as predominately white or predominately black anything on the base. It was just army.

From the very beginning, I was exposed to adults and children who were not only black or white, but who were from all types of ethnic and cultural origins, including Puerto Rican, Catholic, Californian, Mexican, urban, Jewish, and many others. Some of the kids' fathers were officers and some of the kids' fathers were privates.

I knew biracial kids before it became the new minority group in our country. Many of the children I went to school with and lived next to were biracial, with mothers who were German or Japanese who had married black or white American soldiers. In fact, we even lived in Europe for a few years, so I had exposure to other countries, their citizens, and their customs. The terms diversity and multiculturalism had not yet become popular, but I truly lived in a multicultural and culturally diverse environment.

When my dad retired from the army and settled down in Texas, my primary social and educational influences had come from living the military life. Hence, when I started school in that small Texas town, I had army brat cultural characteristics and influences that were different from the other students' backgrounds. I now know my many army cultural influences made it quite easy for me to adjust and even excel in this new environment.

The first army cultural influence to note was my comfort level in being in new and strange environments with new people. This had come from years of practice at being the new kid in the classroom. As an army family, we moved frequently, and I changed schools just as frequently. I enjoyed getting to know all kinds of people and the special attention I received because I was the new kid in class. So I had years of being around individuals who were culturally different from me.

Secondly, I had experience building relationships with all types of kids, teachers, and other people, so adjusting to a new environment really was no big deal. I remember wanting to make new friends and get involved with new groups, clubs, and organizations. My best friend in first grade was white; in the second grade, black and Japanese; in the third grade, white and German; in the fourth grade, black; in the fifth grade, Puerto Rican; in the sixth grade, white; and in the seventh grade, black.

Thirdly, I had no personal memories or painful experiences to hinder my efforts. I had no seriously negative experiences to make me uncomfortable being different. I did not have any major preconceived judgments or psychological baggage to cloud my thoughts with anger, fear, or mistrust. I had not been called any racial slurs. I did not recall anyone treating me badly because of my color or race.

I am sure some of this happened at one time or another, but either I did not notice or I did not care, because I certainly didn't remember. I knew I was black and was proud to be black. I loved and embraced what was known then as Black American culture. This was before the term "African American" was introduced.

I remember singing the James Brown song, "Say It Loud: I'm Black and I'm Proud," and screaming at my first Jackson 5 concert. I also remember grieving the loss of Dr. Martin Luther King Jr. Although being black at the time was an important cultural influence, it was just one of my many influences, and with respect to socializing and working with others, it was not an obstacle but a value.

My dad was stationed in France for a year, and my family decided to stay in the United States. We lived in my mom's home state of Louisiana until my dad returned. For the first time in my life, I attended a segregated school. We attended a black Catholic church, lived in a black neighborhood, and sat in the black balcony of the movie theater.

The interesting thing was that my army cultural influences still dominated my perspectives, experiences, beliefs, and values. I was different from everyone else. Although I looked like the others, I was viewed and treated like I was the outsider, even though we were all black. To this black cultural group, I talked differently, dressed differently, and acted differently. I remember the black teacher even treating me differently from the other students. But yet, I adjusted.

I simply believed that everyone was different. They had different histories, beliefs, values, and pains. I knew different people liked to do different things, go different places, and eat different foods. I always thought of myself as the new kid who simply had to learn about others and how to adjust to others so I could achieve what I wanted.

The fourth army cultural influence I had acquired was a military like work ethic. I learned and appreciated discipline, competition, punctuality, initiative, and working hard to get what I wanted. I also learned the value of proving myself and my abilities to others. I learned early in life that because everyone is different there are no cookie-cutter approaches to people.

Instead, you have to be willing to learn about yourself and others. You have to be willing to gain a certain level of self-acceptance and the acceptance of others. And sometimes you have to learn how to adjust to accomplish your goals. You have to learn how to work with different people in different environments if you are going to succeed in life, while remaining true to yourself. And many times, you have to take responsibility for what happens in your life.

I realize I was just a kid, and kids are often sheltered from the harsh realities of life. I know there was prejudice and discrimination on army bases. Undoubtedly, I was a victim many times without knowing it. But sometimes the best lessons are learned through the eyes of a child.

This story sets the stage for what I believe to be the necessary and fundamental skills and characteristics that will help individuals who have dominating cultural influences. I believe it provides the basic principles for individuals who think primary cultural influences play a large part in their progression toward a leadership position. This story should help you see how you can achieve success in a new environment, including the world of work.

For me, the army provided that opportunity. The army made the physical integration of people from different backgrounds part of the regular process. They provided the basic training, exposure, and practice.

But the army, as with every institution, cannot change another person's feelings, attitudes and beliefs about others simply by putting that person in the same place as others from different cultures. Changing someone's mind and heart has to come from within and is based on what a person does with that opportunity.

No matter how much you know and how good you are at what you do, it is difficult to become successful without learning how to build relationships and work with others. It is crucial that people get to know you and learn to appreciate and respect you. It is equally crucial that you get to know others and learn how to appreciate and respect others. And, if successful, you eventually begin to help each other succeed.

Relationships have to be developed, groomed, and nurtured. You have to adjust so you become comfortable at being the different or new kid on the block. Note I said adjust, not change your identity, give up your beliefs or values, blend in, or and become just like the others.

You have to welcome the challenges you may have to overcome because you are different, along with the challenges you may have due to the corporation's expectations of their employees. You have to have a disciplined, tough, and committed work ethic because achieving success is difficult enough, but achieving success with cultural barriers adds a new dimension to making it in corporate America.

I hope you seek an employer that is proactive and trying to address the needs of a diverse workforce. But you cannot wait for the organization to do all of the changing because, in most cases, you will be losing valuable time. It is unrealistic to expect that any organization is going to change to meet the needs of everyone's cultural influences. By waiting, you will lose the time it takes to develop the skills to become an effective multicultural leader.

Lastly, it is up to you to deal with any psychological baggage you may be carrying around. Anger and resentment from injustices are real and can be powerful. But these feelings and the resultant behaviors can be debilitating and detrimental to future relationships and success if held onto and used unwisely. There is a difference between being uncomfortable in a situation and being fearful in a situation. There is a difference between being disappointed and being angry. There is a difference between being functional and being miserable.

Sometimes such psychological baggage can be unhealthy and even dangerous to your physical and mental health and personal well-being. Powerful and negative feelings, memories, and thoughts should be addressed and dealt with. For some individuals, this may even require formal psychological help or spiritual counseling. It is easy to take such feelings into the wrong places and at the wrong times. It is also up to every individual to make sure there is no harmful baggage being carried into relationships and situations. It often is inappropriate and ineffective in helping one to achieve a leadership position.

6

Multicultural Leadership Development

After a history of affirmative action requirements, cultural diversity training programs, leadership training, and coaching and mentoring programs, many human resources professionals, company executives, and mid-level managers continue to struggle with retaining and promoting their culturally diverse leadership candidates.

In addition, these leaders and HR professionals have had to deal with related diversity issues, including:

- Buy-in and support from executives
- Personal and professional commitment from potential candidates
- Organizational strategic commitment to promotion and retention of candidates
- Development of culturally sensitive leadership programs
- Effective recruiting
- Culturally sensitive leadership skills training programs

Fortunately, many HR professionals and corporate executives are beginning to understand the complexity and necessity of not only a diverse workforce and management team, but also the need for an effective diverse senior management and executive team. They now understand and accept that multicultural leadership is neither just a legal mandate nor a social mandate. They are aware that it is a business mandate.

Now more than ever, we live and work in a society that is made up of multicultural consumers, service providers, competition, vendors, college graduates and other potential employees, and communities. Organizations that want to be successful in a multicultural society must consider multicultural leadership as a major part of having a competitive advantage. For multicultural leadership development to be successful, it has to be part of the corporation's vision, mission, and worldview, as well as its strategic plan.

A culturally inclusive organization is progressive and proactive about diversity. Although hiring and promoting culturally diverse employees is critically important, diversity initiatives have many other facets. Today, successful organizations have diversity requirements, objectives, and goals throughout the organization, including:

- Reaching out to the culturally diverse community and customer base with financial assistance, as well as appropriate goods and services

- Seeking procurement of goods and services from culturally diverse vendors

- Infusing diversity goals within employee and management appraisals

- Reducing discrimination claims and legal actions

- Developing international and global initiatives

- Including diversity initiatives in all advertisements and marketing plans

- Creating a culturally sensitive public image and public relations campaigns
- Achieving salary equity and benefits
- Providing effective training, education, and skill-development programs
- Offering effective personal growth and development programs
- Implementing inclusive long-term succession planning
- Developing culturally sensitive company branding

Leaders of successful organizations know they have to do more than just talk. They have to be able to measure their effectiveness with numbers. They know a diversity plan's effectiveness can be measured in many ways, including:

- The cost of employee turnover
- The cost of recruitment and training
- The value of richer pools of talent and retention
- The importance of broader customer resources
- The value of improved public and community image
- The value of diverse experience, skills, and productivity
- The value of commitment, motivation, and productivity
- The value of effective succession planning and advancement implementation
- The value of diverse procurement programs

An advantage to successful multicultural leadership development is the increased motivation of and commitment from employees who perceive that they will be treated fairly. Another advantage should be profitability from attracting more customers. A third advantage is that the organization can better respond to the needs of the local community and become more representative of wider society.

Organizational Comfort

The potential leadership candidates must have sincere desire, intense preparation, and solid personal commitment. Job-related skills, experience, and expertise are only half the challenge. The multicultural leadership candidate often has to go beyond academic knowledge and prior success. They have to develop effective levels of organizational comfort.

Organizational comfort is like the comfort you feel at home and with your family. When you are at home, you know your way around the house. You know when and how things operate. You know which rooms, and at what times, you can and cannot enter. You are able to talk with family members with ease in a language you all understand. You can relax or be stressed, and you are able to take risks. You are able to be yourself yet still accomplish what you need to accomplish. You are comfortable with yourself and with others. Insecurity, mistrust, fear, and anxiety are minimal and manageable.

When an employee is uncomfortable, for whatever reason, the connections needed to advance in the organization are often not made. Organizational comfort is learning and understanding the unspoken rules and how to quickly navigate the company.

Organizational comfort is learning about and understanding the power structure and the people in power. Organizational comfort is developing confidence in working within that power structure and the extending structure of the organization.

When an employee is uncomfortable in a work environment, it is a matter of time before she becomes complacent and unproductive. The uncomfortable employee may choose to isolate and avoid the very situations, people, and responsibilities needed to advance in an organization. If this discomfort exists long enough, she may become frustrated, impatient, and even angry when it becomes apparent that she is being passed up for promotions or is not being recognized for her contributions.

When another organization offers this individual the slightest opportunity for advancement or increased pay, it is easy for that employee to leave. Often, comfort leads to commitment, and commitment is the only thing that can compete with a better financial offer from another organization. When a person is comfortable and therefore happier with their existing environment, the amount of money can become a secondary incentive.

The trick here is that when an organization is truly culturally diverse, comfort to one person can be different than comfort to another. Cultural comfort cannot be taught in a two-week course. It is not the sole responsibility of the organization and existing leadership team, nor is it the sole responsibility of the individual. Developing cultural comfort should be a goal for both the organization and the leadership candidate.

For the leadership candidate, developing organizational comfort must be an aggressive personal and professional campaign in multicultural leadership development. This campaign should include work-related skills and job performance, but this is only part of what will be required to advance in most organizations. This campaign should also include:

- Multicultural relationship building skills
- Multicultural knowledge and sensitivity
- Multicultural networking and social skills
- Personal and organizational leadership skills

- Multicultural group negotiation and collaboration skills

- Knowledge and understanding of the organization's culture

Effective multicultural leadership must be understood and implemented as a systematic developmental process. It must have personal, social, and institutional elements. True multicultural leadership development must be a three-part process designed for the existing leadership team and the potential leadership candidates of all cultural influences. Those processes are

Part One: Multicultural Self-Awareness and Growth
Part Two: Multicultural Awareness of Others
Part Three: Multicultural Leadership Skill Development and Adjustment

The parts can and should be worked on simultaneously. Becoming an effective multicultural leader requires continuous growth and development and is never-ending. Cultures change, people change, values change, interests change, and competencies change. Therefore, people should always work on developing their self-awareness, learning about others, and improving their skills to be an effective multicultural leader.

7

Multicultural Self-Awareness and Growth

To examine, develop, and facilitate an effective multicultural leadership agenda, the contributing factors to diversity workplace problems must be explored. Many employees, advocates, and the media are quick to point fingers at popular, yet sometimes valid, contributors.

Blame for diversity concerns is frequently placed on society, corporate executives, the government, and even some cultures. Accountability and responsibility for diversity initiatives and compliance seem to lie outside of the company, such as with the government or society, or inside the company, such as with the leaders or departments. It is often quite easy to blame and find fault in what everyone else is or is not doing to deal with the issue.

It makes sense to look for all of the possible causes of the problems. Some causes may be external, while others may be internal. But the organization and society at large are not the only places we need to explore. Individuals in all levels of the organization, including the leadership candidates, potential leaders, and those aspiring for promotion, must learn to look internally for possible contributors to the problems. Everyone, especially leadership candidates, needs to examine what he is doing to contribute to an effective multicultural leadership initiative.

Whether we like it or not or accept it or not, everyone has preconceived notions about others. Because of our unique multicultural backgrounds and influences, we have thoughts and feelings about ourselves and others.

These thoughts and feelings come from many sources. Some may be accurate and valid, such as personal experience, but others may be invalid, such as hearsay, a biased or angry great-grandpa, or a fictional story from TV. These thoughts and feelings may be positive or negative, but they still exist. These preconceived notions will surface, especially when we are around people or situations that we are unfamiliar with or that make us feel uncomfortable. Unfortunately, we are often unaware they exist, unaware when they surface, and unaware of how much power they have over our thoughts, feelings, and behavior.

The impact of our cultural influences shows up all of the time. This is the result of being in the human race. Cultural influences show up in how we do things, how we make things, and how we celebrate. We can see our cultural influences in how we talk to ourselves and others, and how we talk about others. Cultural influences tell us who we are, how we feel about ourselves, and our attitudes about others and situations.

Cultural influences also tell us what is important to us, what we like and dislike, how to behave alone, how to build relationships and treat others, and how to behave in different environments. Cultural influences tell us how to communicate, how to have fun, how to work, how to love, and how to hate.

Cultural influences can come from being a particular race, sex, age, nationality, or religion. They also can come from experiences, events, education, and history. Cultural influences can come from a chosen profession, work departments, social organizations, socioeconomic status, and political affiliations. Many cultural influences are regional, such as rural or urban, or geographical, such as northern or coastal. And of course, individuals can be influenced by a neighborhood, community, family, and friends. The list is endless.

Becoming culturally self-aware is an active process that is always changing and evolving. It requires a never-ending search for information, understanding, insight, and growth. You must study and examine your own cultural influences and be willing to acknowledge how you were influenced in the past and how you are influenced today.

Prejudice

It is natural to put ourselves in the middle of our world and believe everyone else revolves around us. It is also easy to think that the way we see things is the way others see things. We may even think that our way is the only way. But this way of thinking and feeling is often unfair and inappropriate. Unfortunately, it can follow us everywhere we go and show up in everything we do. And unless we really take a look inside, we may not realize how much these cultural influences affect us and others every day.

Everyone has prejudices, stereotypes, and judgments. What must be realized is that a prejudice is simply a feeling one has about a person based on limited information about that person or their cultural groups without considering what is true. A prejudice can be positive or negative. The point is that it exists. If you have limited knowledge about a person, then you are already acting on those thoughts and feelings. If you are not careful, your prejudices can interfere with your effectiveness at work.

Stereotypes

A stereotype is a rigid thought or image about a person or group of people based on limited knowledge about that person or that person's cultural influences. Again, a stereotype can be positive or negative, but they exist within all of us, especially when we are developing perceptions about something or someone we know little about.

It is human nature to have preconceived thoughts about someone from the first moment we see them. When you see someone for the first time, before speaking a word to each other, you already are generating thoughts and feelings about that person. If you don't know anything else about a person other than what you see or have heard, the only thing you can base your thoughts and feelings on is what you already know. These prejudices and stereotypes come from your cultural influences, parents, beliefs, past experiences, or something you heard or saw in the news.

The sooner we admit we have prejudices and stereotypes, the sooner we can examine which thoughts and feelings are productive, realistic, effective, and appropriate and which are not. Everyone has a right to feel and think whatever each one wishes. Ideally, these thoughts and emotions are fair and positive. But sometimes these thoughts and feelings hold us back. Sometimes they keep us from building networks, taking risks, and mastering leadership skills.

What an individual does with these thoughts and feelings can be discouraging, hurtful, or disrespectful. The associated behaviors and actions can be ineffective or debilitating to one's career. And sometimes these behaviors are unfair and even illegal. The impact of prejudices and stereotypes also can influence our workplace decisions and relationships, and ultimately our future within an organization.

Discrimination

Behaviors based on prejudices and stereotyping can result in discrimination. Discrimination is treating someone differently or unfairly based on perceptions, prejudices, stereotypes, and other biased information. When a person is treated unfairly, whether it is overt or covert, it can significantly impact their happiness, productivity, relationships, commitment, performance, morale, and success. It also affects the rest of the organization, including the people and profits.

As individuals, leaders in the organization, and potential candidates for leadership positions, we must thoroughly examine what we think and feel about people who are different. We have to be open and honest with ourselves about our cultural influences, the messages we have learned, the beliefs we agree with, and the things we do.

We must honestly appraise what we think and feel and whether those thoughts and feelings are fair and accurate. If we find we are thinking and feeling unfairly or inaccurately, we must reevaluate and perhaps change. It is impossible to be fair in our actions if our thoughts and feelings are unfair.

Having negative feelings and thoughts about a person is only part of the problem. We must learn to manage these feeling and thoughts so they do not cause us to hurt someone's feelings, insult someone, avoid someone, or treat someone unfairly. To properly manage and change the feelings and thoughts, we have to be aware of and honest about their existence.

People also may be carrying around psychological baggage from their cultural group's history, past experiences, or significant life events. We sometimes buy into things we have heard from others and carry them around in our own experiences or situations. This information can be valuable, but sometimes it can affect our ability to function effectively at work and with others. We may have been hurt in the past and have subsequently become angry, bitter, or untrusting.

As a potential candidate for multicultural leadership, you may be blocking your own success by holding onto old or inappropriate and ineffective psychological baggage. You may be taking your anger, resentment, fear, and anxiety with you wherever you go. Your cultural baggage may be the reason you cannot build effective relationships, work in teams, or network effectively. It is easy to blame the organization or other people, but it is much more difficult to look inside and discover how we may be contributing to the problem ourselves.

In some cases, you may have to seek help from a trusted and objective friend, educator, spiritual advisor, or mental health professional. Depending on the thoughts and feelings, it may take considerable time for you to address and overcome your issues. But it would be unfair for you to want others to understand you, value you, and make appropriate changes if you are not willing to understand yourself, value yourself, and also make appropriate changes within yourself.

More importantly, an organization cannot be a leader in diversity if its employees' hearts and minds are not on the same level. Corporations can facilitate the best diversity and inclusion programs, but if the employees do not do their part, disagree with underlying principles, or undermine the program's basic philosophy and goals, the diversity efforts are meaningless. A diversity-driven corporate culture must be inclusive of diversity-driven people.

Taking a hard look is not just about thoughts and feelings. It is also about values. At times, individuals may know and accept that they have a negative or inappropriate thought or feeling about a person or group, and for whatever reason, they do not want to adjust accordingly. Other times, they may feel that their prejudices and stereotypes are justified or of personal value.

This is when it is time for even more critical evaluation. Leadership candidates should look at their values and compare them to the organization's values, culture, and diversity goals. They have to ask themselves whether they are being true to themselves, as well as to the organization, and whether they are being ethical or hypocritical.

It is unfair to ask an organization to adjust to the needs of its diverse workforce without the workforce making adjustments too. A company cannot be unbiased and culturally sensitive when the individuals are unwilling to do the same. The organization can provide information, guidance, direction, opportunity, and experiences, but it cannot make its members adjust. The employees have to be willing to take that step. If they aren't, then perhaps they should consider finding an organization that is better suited to their personal, professional, and cultural values.

8

Multicultural Awareness of Others

Multicultural leadership development must include learning about other cultural groups and influences. Sometimes a person's behaviors and beliefs are significantly influenced by one cultural group more than any other. In these situations or relationships, it can be beneficial to learn about the values, beliefs, and customs of such groups.

If an individual ascribes to a particular cultural group's beliefs, values, and expectations, it is valuable and culturally sensitive to learn as much as possible about that group. Of course, you should not assume any cultural group's influence; ask for verification first.

For example, a person may look like she is of Japanese decent, but she may have been born and raised in America and know nothing about Japanese culture. It would have been inaccurate to assume that the person ascribed to traditional Japanese customs. However, if you know a person follows traditional Japanese customs and beliefs, just think how much better your relationship could be by knowing more about what is important or meaningful to her.

Cultures vary in many ways. It would be impossible to adequately explain about each one. But I can give you enough information to get you started. You have to continually seek out information, research, and get to know different cultures and perspectives. To become a culturally skilled leader is a never-ending process.

When learning about other cultural groups, it is important to distinguish between traditional characteristics and practices and current characteristics and practices. Depending on the person, either or both areas may be important to research and understand.

The most obvious ways cultures vary are in physical characteristics, languages, dress, and history. Other cultural differences include religious beliefs and practices, political views, family values, and rules. All of these are extremely important areas to learn about.

Cultures also vary from one another in:

- Work ethic
- Material values
- Present and historic beliefs and values
- Group orientation and beliefs about collaboration and individualism
- Practices in building work relationships, including views of organizational hierarchy
- Nature and spirituality
- Verbal and nonverbal communication patterns and rules
- Family, community, and social hierarchy
- Economic and class beliefs and values
- Gender-related beliefs and values
- Age-related beliefs and values
- Political structures

There are also more subtle ways that cultural influences can affect an individual, such as thinking, working, and emotional styles; value of marital status and profession; sexual orientation; and mental and physical abilities.

Some cultural differences may vary from traditional corporate cultural values:

- The corporate culture may value individualism and personal goals, whereas other cultures may value group accomplishments and goals.

- Corporate communication skills are often valued when they are immediate, open, personal, verbal, and public. Other cultures may respect silence, nonverbal communication, building rapport, and private communication.

- Strategic plans often emphasize long-range, ambiguous planning and goal-setting for individuals, whereas many cultural groups respect short-term, concrete, and immediate approaches to goal accomplishment.

- The corporation may value controlling nature and science, while many cultures believe it is inappropriate to control nature, but that it is to be honored and respected.

- Beliefs and practices of religion, male-female relationships, attire, and celebrations, rewards, and recognitions at work may all differ.

- Some cultural groups see the manager or supervisor as the respected expert to provide instructions and answers, rather than a person with whom to openly and honestly discuss matters.

These are just a few examples of how cultural groups can vary. But you can see how important it is to learn as much as possible about an individual's primary cultural influences and how they can impact that person in the workplace.

This knowledge is essential for you to become a successful multicultural leader and to gain multicultural comfort. It is especially needed to build successful multicultural relationships. And lastly, this information may help others build organizational comfort in being who they are, as well as being a viable contributor to the organization.

Aside from formal research and traveling to other parts of the world, one of the best ways to learn about a person's cultural influences is simply to get to know the person and ask questions. Genuine and sincere interest with respectful curiosity and without prejudgment and criticism is usually understood and appreciated. Of course, this is different from being nosy, impolite, and inappropriately personal and intrusive. Most people who are proud of their cultural influences love to talk about their family, customs, country, and beliefs. People generally want to be properly understood, appreciated, and valued.

One of the worst things you can do is avoid the person and avoid talking about what is important to them. It is not worth the risk to make inaccurate assumptions and possible cultural errors. At the same time, it is equally important to help others understand you and your cultural differences and values. This is not the time to isolate and be secretive. This will only build walls between you and others in the organization. You have to be willing to share about yourself and learn about others. It is a two-way process.

Multicultural leaders must take cultural risks and help others take cultural risks to be perceived as trustworthy and able to lead others effectively. Two-way information sharing, when done appropriately, is the key to becoming culturally sensitive and skilled, as well as building multicultural trust, organizational comfort, and leadership skills.

9

Multicultural Leadership Skill Development and Adjustment

The third part of the multicultural leadership development process is the acquisition of skills that are required for organizational success. The goal is to have a significant level of corporate comfort so you are a viable part of the system and are able to build relationships, take risks, and be successful leading others.

When corporate comfort is acquired, it is easier to gain the knowledge, experience, and confidence needed to take risks, build relationships, and develop multicultural leadership competence. These tools make the difference between knowing how to do a good job and being able to make it to the top.

Developing effective multicultural leadership skills will require an assessment of your current skills. You should ask yourself the following questions:

- How do I feel about myself, my cultural influences, and the people I work with?

- Am I willing to speak up about an injustice to myself or others?

- Do I know my strengths and weaknesses?

- Do I have baggage that I haven't dealt with? How does it affect my work?

- Am I having trouble balancing my personal life with my work life?

- Do I have support from family and friends?

- What makes me angry, bothered, or upset? How do these feeling affect me at work?

- Am I comfortable and willing to take risks? If not, why and what will make it better?

- Am I willing to ask for help? If not, why and what will make it easier?

- In what areas do I need formal training?

- In what areas do I need more practice?

- Do I agree with the ethical principles and behaviors of the organization and the people I work with? How does that affect my work?

- Beyond being good at what I do, am I ready to lead a multicultural work group?

- What is it about being a multicultural leader that is important to me?

- How am I different from other employees in the way I work with others? How am I similar?

- What have I done that has worked and not worked?

- Do I need to learn how to network better?

- Do I know and understand the culture of the organization? the department? the community? the customer? my workforce?

- Do I know, understand, and agree with the organization's politics, policies, and laws?

- Do I know and understand the organization's structure, mission, and goals?

- Do I know how to build relationships with people in various levels of the organization?

- Do I isolate myself, avoid certain people and situations, and keep my thoughts to myself?

- Do I struggle with language and communication barriers?

- Do I listen without prejudgment?

- Do others struggle with my language and communication style?

- Do I understand the verbal and nonverbal communication patterns and styles of others in the organization?

- Do I know and understand what is expected of a leader in this organization?

These are just some of the questions that will help you to determine how much work you have ahead of you. Upon making an assessment, it is up to you to fill in the gaps. You should work to overcome deficiencies and build on strengths. It won't happen overnight, but it can happen.

Corporate Cultural Continuum©

I have a theory called the Corporate Cultural Continuum©. In the diagram on Page 47, the horizontal line represents a continuum. I believe everyone in an organization is somewhere different on that continuum.

Low Organizational Comfort

On the extreme left side of the continuum, you will find the individuals who have dominating cultural influences that are extremely different from the individuals who are considered mainstream within the organization. These individuals probably know very little about the corporate culture and do not have the needed relationships, communication skills, or leadership skills. They probably have very little organizational comfort.

This position on the continuum has little to do with an individual's job skills or ability to perform. This person can be the best at what he does. The farther to the left a person is on this continuum, the more personal, interpersonal, and multicultural leadership skill development adjustments he will have to make.

High Organizational Comfort

On the extreme right side of the continuum, you will find the individuals who are comfortable, knowledgeable, and skilled within the corporate culture. They know how to navigate the organization and develop the needed networks and relationships. They have corporate cultural knowledge and leadership skills, take risks, and get promoted or recognized easily.

However, these people will also have to make some adjustments to become great multicultural corporate leaders. They may be so entrenched in the corporate culture that they know, understand, and value little about the cultural needs of the organization, the workforce, the customers, or the business. They may be good organizational leaders but perhaps are insensitive, biased, or simply unaware of the value of a culturally diverse organization.

The existing leadership team must make the necessary adjustments because they have the power to develop multicultural leadership opportunities and programs. The corporate leaders set the tone and the policy for the future of the multicultural organization. It does no good to have a diversity initiative without support, understanding, and commitment from the current leaders.

These same leaders may need to go through the three-part process for multicultural leadership development. They too may need to look inside, learn about others, and develop new skills.

The adjustment level for the individual at the far right is generally lower than the adjustment level for the individual at the far left. This is because the need for the business to be profitable still exists. The person with less corporate comfort will have to make the most adjustments. Usually this person has the most cultural differences from the main-stream leadership and leadership candidates. If these individuals do not make necessary adjustments, the organization will not make necessary adjustments. Hence, everyone needs to make some adjustments to develop a multicultural organization with multicultural leadership.

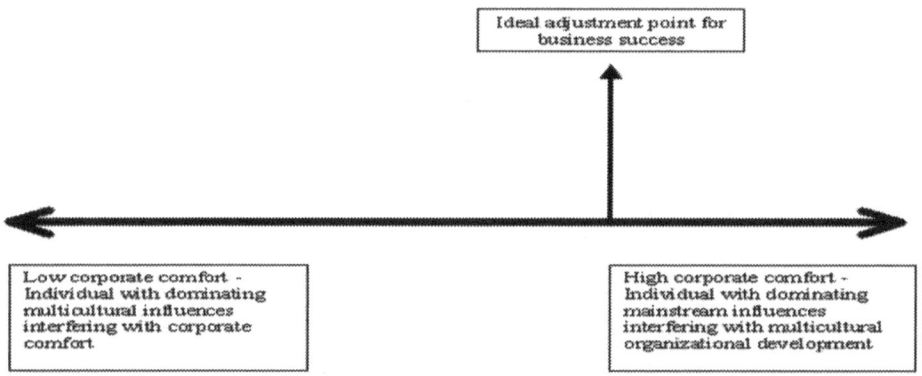

The theory behind the Corporate Cultural Continuum© involves the following thoughts:

1. Due to the complexity of an individual's multiple cultural influences, no two people are alike, therefore each person is multicultural. Some cultural influences are more dominating than others. Therefore, everyone is at a different place on the continuum. Some are extremely to the left, some are more in the middle, and some are more to the right.

2. Every leader and potential leader in the organization may need to make adjustments to meet the needs of the business and to ensure the success of a diverse and multicultural leadership team and organization.

10

The Multicultural Leadership Development Process

Effective multicultural leadership development is a process-oriented program. It can be completed by an individual, but ideally it should be a joint effort between the organization, the leadership candidates, and the existing leadership team. It is a long-term training, coaching, and developmental process that takes time to learn, practice, and evaluate.

A good multicultural leadership development process combines several components:

- Culturally focused leadership training
- Culturally focused coaching and counseling
- Personal and organizational psychological principles
- Personal and business management assessments, research, and measurements

A good program curriculum will include discussions on topics such as:

- Corporate culture and barriers to success
- Bicultural stress and balancing life
- Trust and mistrust

- Cultural identity
- Relationship and group orientation
- Cultural activity, work ethic, and time orientation
- Multicultural management strategies
- Cultural values and corporate expectations
- Transition and change
- Networking skills
- Coping skills
- Negotiation skills
- Social skills
- Corporate barriers and personal limitations

Everyone has multicultural influences that make us unique, so cookie-cutter approaches or short training courses will not work. There is no quick fix. Developmental change takes time for thinking, feeling, and growing. We must learn to develop the whole person from their worldview. Only an ongoing process will produce sustainable results.

An effective organizational program can provide:

- Increased number of qualified and skilled executive candidates
- Increased retention rates of diverse managers
- Improved diversity climate and relationships
- Enhanced manager commitment and performance
- Improved employee, public, and customer perceptions of diversity and diversity commitment.

An effective personal program can provide:

- Enhanced personal and professional growth

- Improved collaboration and negotiation skills

- Strengthened leadership skills across cultural lines

- Improved understanding of corporate culture

Multicultural leadership development is an aggressive campaign. It is an investment in yourself, your organization, and your future.

Contact Dr. Pam Johnson for
speaking, consulting, coaching
and training services:
1-972-997-8225
pjohnson@ncdperformance.com

978-0-595-38518-8
0-595-38518-4

www.ingramcontent.com/pod-product-compliance
Lightning Source LLC
Chambersburg PA
CBHW021020180526
45163CB00005B/2047